POP★PEOPLE™

HANSON
101 COOL QUESTIONS

by Michael-Anne Johns

SCHOLASTIC INC.

New York   Toronto   London   Auckland   Sydney
Mexico City   New Delhi   Hong Kong

Front Cover: South Beach Photo; Back Cover: South Beach Photo; Page 1: South Beach Photo; Page 2: (top) Caroline Torem-Craig/London Features; Page 2: (bottom) Paul Smith/Retna; Page 3: Caroline Torem-Craig/London Features; Page 4: David Allocca/DMI; Page 6: South Beach Photo; Page 7: George Desota/London Features.

ISBN 0-439-23325-9

12 11 10 9 8 7 6 5 4 3 2 1   0 1 2 3 4 5/0

Printed in the U.S.A.
First Scholastic printing, September 2000

GUIDE TO WHAT'S INSIDE

Hanson Intro

They're ba-a-a-a-ack!

That's right. Unless you've been hiding out on a desert island (and going to Leonardo Di-Caprio's *The Beach* doesn't count), you are very aware that Hanson — brothers Isaac, Taylor, and Zac — is back on the music scene. The boys are hipper and hotter than ever — This Time Around! If this is your first time around with Hanson, here's what you need to know.

Times They Are a 'Changin'

The boys from Tulsa, Oklahoma, became famous with the release of the first single, "MMMBop," from their multiplatinum debut album, *Middle of Nowhere*. For nearly six months, "MMMBop" was all you heard on the radio, on MTV, on Walkmans, and on CD players all over the country. Even Isaac (better known as Ike), Taylor (better known as Tay), and Zac (better known as "the maniac") realized the world had gone "MMM-Bop" crazy when their hit single was remixed into elevator Musak. The brothers even apeared on *Saturday Night Live* in a parody of "MMM-Bop" overkill. The unfortunate result of "MMM-Bop" was that too many people dismissed Hanson as pure bubblegum sugar.

Now, don't feel sorry for the brothers from America's heartland — they "MMMBop"ed all the way to the bank. But along the way, a lot of people overlooked the fact that the then sixteen-year-old Ike, fourteen-year-old Tay, and ten-year-old Zac were really good musicians, that they actually wrote most of their own songs, played instruments, and could harmonize like angels. Even though they released other successful albums — the 1997 Christmas album, *Snowed In*, and 1998's collection of early demos, *3 Car Garage*, and the live album, *Live from Albertane* — Hanson seemed to disappear from the radio radarscope after that.

There were unverified sightings; there were queries as to what had happened to Hanson. Well, the fact is Ike, now nineteen, Taylor, seventeen, and Zac, fourteen, grew up! Ike and Taylor cut their hair. Ike got rid of his braces. And Zac sprouted like a weed.

And they released a brand-new album, *This Time Around*. They are older, definitely wiser, and on the cutting edge of a whole new cycle in music. Their sound is more mature, more rock-influenced, truer to the music they were raised with — 1950s and 1960s rock and roll.

One thing hasn't changed, though — an interview with Ike, Tay, and Zac is never uneventful. Try as Ike and Tay might to be a calming influence on little bro Zac, he still pops up with some outrageous moments. Take, for example, when the three were doing a *Teen People* photo shoot to promote *This Time Around*. Taylor was trying to explain how they click as a group. "We all trade off roles," he said. "For instance, at times Zac can be psychotic, and at other times totally linear, like, 'Shut up, we gotta work on this.' If you're trying to describe what role we play, we all play every role."

Then Zac had to add his own two cents — "If we did fight, we all know *I'd* be the only one left standing!"

Luckily for Hanson fans, the three are all standing — onstage and performing. And, after almost three years, ready to answer all your questions. We have 101 of them, so check out what Ike, Tay, and Zac have to say!

1
Brotherly Love

Isaac, Taylor, and Zac reveal answers to some family questions!

1. Who is the most romantic of the brothers?
Taylor: "Ike, definitely — he's always going on about girls. He always writes letters and songs about them!"

2. Do Zac's parents or brothers treat him differently now that he is a teenager?
Zac: "No, I'm not really treated any differently. I've always been treated the same way. We really don't treat each other like we're different ages.

As far as I'm concerned, I'm eighteen and Ike is two."

3. What are the names of Hanson's parents and brothers and sisters?

Clarke Isaac, Jordan Taylor, and Zachary Walker Hanson are the three oldest sons of Diana and Walker Hanson. The younger Hanson siblings are sisters Jessica, Avery, and Zoe and brother Mackenzie.

4. Are Jessica, Avery, Zoe, or Mackenzie musically inclined? Will any of them join the band?

Taylor: "I'd be surprised if our younger sisters or brother join the band — they could set up one of their own, though. . . . We don't want to put them too much in the spotlight [right now]."
Ike: "The whole family is involved in our music. They have to listen to it all the time, and they always travel with us to see our live gigs."

5. What was the worst fight Isaac, Taylor, and Zac have ever had?

Taylor: "We don't fight very much at all. We spend so much time together that there seems to be less of an age gap between us."

Ike: "We [fight] occasionally. We've had fights when we were younger where we've nearly killed each other!"

Taylor: "Once I got Zac so wound up that he dragged me around the [room] by my hair!"

Zac: "We were play-fighting [a couple of years ago], and I broke my nose. We were all wrestling together and I fell. I don't know whether it was Taylor or Ike, because we were all wrestling together."

6. When they do have disagreements, do they hold grudges?

Taylor: "No. Being in a band together makes it even better, because we know each other so well. It's, like, you're gonna argue, then it's over, and you're still together. What are you gonna do? Walk across the room and pout?"

Ike: "You still gotta rehearse."

7. There are so many Hanson kids, have any of them ever been left behind by accident?

Zac: "[Mackenzie] was left behind at a gas station once. We didn't realize it for two hours, but when we got back to the gas station, the pump guy had looked after him really well. Maybe he didn't miss us at all."

8. What's the best and worst thing about having so many siblings?

Zac: "The best is you never get lonely, and the worst thing is that you can never *be* lonely. There's always someone around."

Ike: "There's always someone around to hang out with, but the worst thing is, well, frankly, we get on so well there's nothing bad about it at all."

9. Are Ike, Taylor, and Zac competitive with one another?

Ike: "I would never really say we're competitive."

Taylor: "Unless you're talking video games."

Ike: "Zac kills us!

Zac: "That's because I've been playing since I was three."

10. Why is Zac known as "the crazy one"?

Zac: "I think it's probably actually that I'm so shy that I just act wacky to make up for it."

Taylor: "He *is* a little crazy! . . . He's dragged people up onstage. [When we first started out] we would give T-shirts away. This one girl raised her hand, but she was too embarrassed to come up, so Zac went out there and carried her onto the stage."

Zac: "I'm just hyper because I'm having a good time. I've got lots of energy. Ike says I'm very strong for a kid my age. But I am normal — sort of!"

Ike: "He freaks people out sometimes because he does these weird voices and he doesn't always answer questions intelligibly. But he surprises people with the way he thinks."

11. Are there any more Hanson siblings planned?

Taylor: "No."

Zac: "I don't know — you'd have to ask our parents."

Ike: "Zoe, our little sister, is two now, and she's quite a handful."

12. How do Ike, Taylor, and Zac describe one another?

It's hard to get the three brothers to be serious about questions like this. During an interview for *This Time Around*, they totally goofed on a reporter.

Taylor: "We hate each other!"

Zac: "We have restrictions. [Taylor] has to stay at least two feet away."

2
Fascinating Faves

Think you're an expert on Ike, Tay, and Zac? If you know the answers to the questions below — you definitely are Hanson-worthy!

13. Does Zac, Taylor, or Isaac have a favorite soda?

Zac's a pepper — he recently confessed to *Rolling Stone* magazine, "I favor Dr Pepper, yes. It's one of the sweeter colas." And according to *Seventeen* magazine, Ike's a pepper, too. But Taylor is a "diet pepper" — when they were talking to a reporter for a 1997 article, that's all they drank! And they have a preference for Jelly Belly Very Cherry jelly beans!

14. When Zac goes on tour, is there one thing he must have with him?

Zac: "I [always] take a Nintendo or a Sony PlayStation to entertain [myself] on the tour bus."

15. Is it true that all the Hanson brothers are major surfers?

Yes. Yes. Yes. Though they didn't get much of a chance to surf in their native Tulsa, Oklahoma — not a lot of waves in a landlocked city — Ike, Taylor, and Zac picked up the sport when they first went to Los Angeles to record *Middle of Nowhere*. Now they hang ten whenever they can. "We really enjoy it, and whenever we get the opportunity, we hit the ocean," Ike said in a recent Yahoo! on-line chat. Zac added, "We assault it — we put the ocean in its place!"

16. Do the guys still listen to 1950s and 1960s music or do they like more current music now?

Ike, Taylor, and Zac like all kinds of music, from old-time rock to gospel. While they were making

This Time Around, Zac and Taylor pointed out that it was hard to listen to anyone other than themselves. However, he does say he likes "all the crows — Counting Crows, Black Crowes, Sheryl Crow — as well as Beck, Lenny Kravitz, and Lauryn Hill." Ike admits that he can't get enough of Carlos Santana's incredible album, *Supernatural,* and Lenny Kravitz's *5*.

17. Does Zac prefer to perform live or to work in the recording studio?

Zac: "The most fun thing is just performing. I was at a show recently, and I was just realizing how much fun it was to be out there in front of the fans, just playing music."

18. What is Hanson's favorite snack when they are in the recording studio?

Ike: "We ate a ton of Chex mix."

Taylor: "Our grandma always made Chex party mix — she wasn't in the studio with us, so we went out and got it in the grocery."

19. Ike collects guitars — does he have a favorite one?

Yes, he does. He bought it in 1999, but it's a vintage 1966 Gibson ES335 — and it's cherry-red. His other prize guitar has special meaning to him. Since Ike is a huge Aerosmith fan, he was quick to purchase a Joe Perry signature guitar — "It has a black sunburst with black curly tiger stripes with an internal wa-wa pedal that Joe Perry created."

20. What are Zac's favorite comic strips?

He loves *Calvin & Hobbes*, but his all-time favorite is *Peanuts*.

21. Since Hanson actually play all their own instruments, other musicians must have influenced them. Who is Taylor's favorite piano player, Zac's favorite drummer, and Ike's favorite guitarist?

Taylor: "As an artist, I'd say Billy Joel — his playing style and songwriting."

Ike: "I'd probably say Chuck Berry. He's kind of the founder of the electric guitar. He's a rock-

14

and-roll icon. I also really admire Jonny Lang because I think he's a great player."

Zac: "As far as drums, I don't have one person I really admire — I just really enjoy a good drummer."

22. Where's the favorite place the guys have visited?

Taylor: "SegaWorld in London was pretty cool because we love playing Laser Quest."

Zac: "No, the best thing was going to a chocolate factory in Germany. There were chocolate fountains that you could dip wafers in and eat them. I'd like to get one for back home!"

23. What are Zac's favorite pig-out snacks?

Zac: "Ding Dongs and Twinkies are my most important food group. And I also like lasagna and hot dogs and pizza and . . ."

24. What is Zac's favorite high-tech toy?

Zac: "We like to play around with digital video cameras and go on the Net."

25. What sports are Hanson's favorites?

Taylor: "We like to play basketball and football, but soccer is a favorite because that's the only one we're halfway good at. And we love to Rollerblade."

26. What's Hanson's favorite kind of fan mail?

Taylor: "Cool letters, like, 'I was doing this and that, and I realized when I heard your music I wanted to do this other thing because you guys are doing what you love.' That's very cool, to be able to inspire people. But you still can't let that stuff go to your head, because it's so fleeting."

27. What is Zac's favorite video game?

Zac is a total gamer and loves to try anything new, but he always reverts to Goldeneye. (Even Ike admits, "Goldeneye is a classic.")

3
Inside Their Date Books

The super scoop about Ike, Tay, and Zac . . . and girls, girls, girls!

28. Do Ike and Taylor ever fight over girls?
Ike: "No. We *definitely* don't fight over girls, but we can't agree on who is cute. You know what's funny, a lot of times when we're onstage, I'll say, 'Oh, I think that girl's cute,' and Taylor will say, 'Oh, I think that girl next to her is cuter.' It [makes things easier], really."

29. When Hanson first became popular, Zac said he thought girls were "yucky" — does he still feel that way?

Zac: "No, it's not 'girls, yuck' anymore, but I don't have anyone special right now. I haven't really gone out on dates yet, because I don't have anyone in mind to ask out. I don't think I've been in love yet."

30. When do you know it's the right time to ask a girl out?

Taylor: "Well, see, at that point, if you're gonna ask someone out for a date, you already know her. It's not like you meet somebody and go, 'Wow, she's hot,' and you ask her out. I want to make friends with her first. [I] want to make sure it's actually about [her] liking [me] as opposed to [her] thinking 'Wow, I'm gonna date a guy from Hanson.' I don't want dating to be something superficial. . . . I'm not seeing anyone right now — no steady girlfriend."

Ike: "You meet all kinds of different people, and I agree with Tay. That's the way it is with us. We try to be friends first, before we ask [a girl] out."

31. What do Isaac, Taylor, and Zac look for in a girl?

Taylor: "I always get asked what kind of girls I think are attractive. I don't have a certain type."

Ike: "I don't have a certain type, either. It's not a good idea. If you have a type then you limit yourself and you might be closing your mind to a wonderful girl who could surprise you."

Zac: "I don't have a girlfriend. That's all in the future for me. I don't know what love is all about yet. I've got to find that out. It should be OK."

32. Does Zac think Ike is a romantic?

Zac: "Ike is a girl charmer. He'll always say nice things to girls. It's just something he does."

33. Has Zac ever kissed a girl?

Zac: "I've never kissed a girl, but I do think about it. And it's not like there's just one type of girl who's right for me, because you say that and then you fall for someone who's the exact opposite of what you said."

34: Has Hanson ever written a song about a real-life girl?

Ike: "Yes."

Taylor: "Most of those girls don't know it — we've written a lot of love songs, and there are many girls who've been in relationships with us that we've written about."

Ike: "I think I gave one girl a cassette tape with songs on it for Valentine's Day — a long time ago."

Zac: "I'd never admit to something like that."

4
Backstage Pass

Here's all the info you need to know about Hanson and their music.

35. Exactly how many CDs has Hanson released?
This Time Around, which was released on May 9, 2000, is Hanson's sixth CD. The following is their complete discography.

INDEPENDENT RELEASE
Boomerang
(1995 — album)
MMMBop
(1996 — album)

LABEL RELEASE:

MMMBop

(1997 — Mercury Records: single)

Tracks:

"MMMBop" (single version)

"MMMBop" (album version)

"MMMBop" (Dust Brothers mix)

"MMMBop" (Hex mix)

Where's the Love

(1997 — Mercury Records: single)

Tracks:

"Where's the Love" (album version)

"Look at You"

"Where's the Love" (Tommy D Landinium dub)

"Where's the Love" (Tommy D Ministry dub)

I Will Come to You

(1997 — Mercury Records: single)

Tracks:

"I Will Come to You"

"Cry"

"MMMBop"

"Madeline" (live)

Weird

(1997 — Mercury Records: single)

Tracks:

"Weird" (album version)

"I Will Come to You (Tee's radio version)

"Speechless"

"I Will Come to You" (Tee's Frozen Club mix)

Middle of Nowhere

(1997 — Mercury Records: album)

Tracks:

"Thinking of You"

"MMMBop"

"Weird"

"Speechless"

"Where's the Love"

"Yearbook Song"

"Lucy"

"I Will Come to You"

"A Minute Without You"

"Madeline"

"With You in Your Dreams"

"Man from Milwaukee" (garage mix)

Snowed In

(1997 — Mercury Records: album)

Tracks:

"Merry Christmas, Baby"

"What Christmas Means to Me"

"Little Saint Nick"

"At Christmas"

"Christmas (Baby, Please Come Home)"

"Rockin' Around the Christmas Tree"

"Christmas Time"

"Everybody Knows the Claus"

"Run, Rudolph, Run"

"Silent Night Medley ('O Holy Night,' 'Silent Night,' 'O, Come, All Ye Faithful')"

"White Christmas"

3 Car Garage

(1998 — Mercury Records: album)

Tracks:

"Day Has Come"

"Two Tears"

"Thinking of You"

"River"

"Surely as the Sun"

"MMMBop"

"Soldier"

"Stories"

"Pictures"

"Sometime"

"With You in Your Dreams"

Live from Albertane

(1998 — Mercury Records: album)

Tracks:

"Gimme Some Lovin'/Shake a Tail Feather"

"Where's the Love"

"River"

"I Will Come to You"

"Ever Lonely"

"Speechless"

"With You in Your Dreams"

"A Minute Without You"

"Money (That's What I Want)"

"More Than Anything"

"MMMBop"

"Man from Milwaukee"

This Time Around

(2000 — Universal Records: album)

Tracks:

"You Never Know"

"If Only"

"This Time Around"

"Runaway Run"

"Save Me"

"Dying to Be Alive"

"Can't Stop"

"Wish That I Was There"

"Love Song"

"Sure About It"

"Hand in Hand"

"In the City"

"A Song to Sing"

36. How is Hanson's new album, *This Time Around,* different from *Middle of Nowhere*?

Isaac explained Hanson's new direction to *Rolling Stone*: "The songs are a little more rock and roll than our other stuff. Some have old R&B and gospel choruses, and we [had] a choir come in. That [was] really fun." Taylor explained in a Yahoo! on-line chat, "The music is still pop music, but I think it's evolved. It's taken a new rock-

and-roll direction. It's still pop music, but it's got an edge that it didn't have before."

37. Hanson seemed to fall off the face of the Earth after *3 Car Garage*. Why did they disappear for so long?

Ike: "I think it was circumstance. If we would have known how things would have gone, we might have changed a little bit of what we did, but I don't think we have any regrets. We did a lot of different things. We did a Christmas record, which was awesome — we really enjoyed doing that, and then we released *3 Car Garage*. We also released a live record and a live video, which was a follow-up to our other long-form video, *Tulsa, Tokyo, and the Middle of Nowhere*. So we have definitely done a lot. Unfortunately, I think people didn't necessarily know about some of the things that we did. So [with *This Time Around*] we wanted to make the best record we could and hope that everybody likes it. We didn't do it quickly."

Taylor: "We thought we'd release it last year. But [now] I think the timing is really good. We've kind of grown up. It's easier to come out with something different, something that's changed and evolved a little bit."

38. Do Ike, Tay, and Zac write all of their songs?

Actually, they have written or cowritten most of their songs — except the traditional songs on their Christmas album, *Snowed In*, and a few tracks of *Live from Albertane*.

39. What is MOE?

MOE is the official Hanson Fan Club and also the name of their official thirty-two-page color magazine. Ike, Taylor, and Zac have a lot of input, and Ike has designed artwork for the magazine. Its seventh edition is coming out, and it includes articles, exclusive contests, and photos. For more information, check out Hanson's official Web site: www.hansonline.com

To coincide with *This Time Around*, Ike explains, "We're doing a special enhanced CD for people in our fan club, MOE. It includes five songs, which are from our previous independent

The brothers Hanson are back! Zac, Ike, and Taylor have a cool new look and a smooth new sound on their latest album, *This Time Around*.

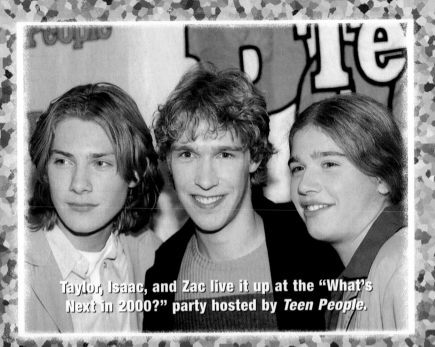

Taylor, Isaac, and Zac live it up at the "What's Next in 2000?" party hosted by *Teen People*.

The brothers paused for fans and photos at the *MTV Video Music Awards* in Los Angeles.

The trio that plays together, sticks together. Even when they fight, the brothers don't hold grudges because, as Ike says, "You still gotta rehearse."

Ike, Tay, and Zac hang with Sisqo (lead singer of Dru Hill), at the Apollo Theater in New York City.

Taylor rocks on the mike, live in concert.

Hanson's new sound is "a little more band, a little more rock 'n' roll, a little less 'poppy,'" explains Taylor, master of the keyboards.

Hanson's new sound made news around the world — "If Only," the first single released overseas, climbed right to the top of the charts in Australia.

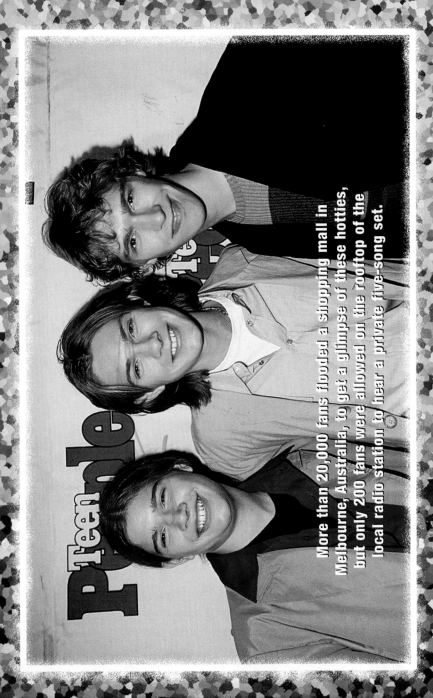

More than 20,000 fans flooded a shopping mall in Melbourne, Australia, to get a glimpse of these hotties, but only 200 fans were allowed on the rooftop of the local radio station to hear a private five-song set.

Hanson is a boy band unlike many others — they don't dance, they do play their own instruments, write their own songs, and even co-produced *This Time Around*. The boys are growing up!

record, and has special computer-related things on it like screen savers and wallpaper and special video clips . . . It's available if you join MOE now or renew your membership."

40. How did Hanson hook up with Jonny Lang and John Popper of Blues Travelers for *This Time Around*?

Taylor: "We actually kind of called [Jonny], because we wanted to meet him. We're big fans of his. We were in London and called and said, 'We're going to see this movie, do you want to come with us?' And he was, like, 'Sure.' So he came down and saw the movie and [we] struck up a little friendship. Then he was in Tulsa playing, and we came and saw him and asked if he wanted to play on our new record. He said sure!

"As for John Popper, we were on tour and were, like, 'Hey, would you ever wanna play on something if we were working on it?' And he was, like, 'Yeah.' So basically, once we started working on *This Time Around*, we called him up and he was there. John Popper is one of the funniest people you'll ever meet. I mean, just totally. He'll totally get you rolling on the ground. He's so funny. A great guy to talk to. You don't often get the opportunity to work with people who are that talented and that good at their craft."

41. Why did Hanson pick the band LarryLand to open for them on tour?

When Hanson was in Europe, they heard this band called LarryLand and really liked them. The group includes singer-songwriter Alan Cronin from Dublin, Ireland, street singer Stanford Vinson from the United States, bassist Nicolai Munch-Hansen, and drummer Casper Hansen from Denmark, and finally, keyboardist Jonas Berg, who's from Sweden. They signed with Triune Music Group, which is the management company that handles Hanson. They released a thirteen-song debut album called *LarryLand*. The album got good reviews, and they hope the Hanson tour will give them the big break they need. Taylor agrees. "It's always fun to be able to help other bands get out there," he told fans in a Yahoo! on-line chat. As a matter of fact, this is not the first time Hanson has given another band a chance. During their *3 Car Garage* minitour, a band named Admiral Twin opened for them. "They're a local band from Tulsa," Taylor says. "We knew them for a long time before we got signed."

42. How does Hanson get their ideas for songs?

Ike: "I think we tend to write about all kinds of different things, and it's whatever comes into your mind. Life is your inspiration. You never know what's going to happen. Some of the songs are about love, about relationships breaking up, some about being crazy about a girl."

Taylor: "We write songs about every facet of life."

43. What's the silliest question Hanson has ever been asked by a reporter?

According to Zac, it definitely was the time a reporter who was doing a phone interview with Hanson asked the boys how they first met!

44. Is it true that Hanson will be in the *Guinness Book of World Records*?

They just might be in the upcoming edition. Previously the record for the loudest rock-and-roll concert was set by The Who. In one concert, the sound level reached 126 decibels. At a 1998 Hanson concert, the sound level was registered at 140 decibels.

45. Is it true that there was a near riot at a Hanson *This Time Around* promotional appearance in Pittsburgh, PA?

Well, it wasn't a riot, but the promoters of their appearance — B94 radio/Adecco Children's Miracle Network radiothon at the Monroeville Mall — expected a possible 750 fans to show up. More than 2,000 screaming fans appeared to hear Hanson sing and watch them play Twister with the radio DJs. Girls from as far away as Canada showed up, and for a time, the thirty-five strong mall guards almost couldn't hold them back!

46. Does Hanson think that American audiences are different from European ones?
Taylor: "It's kind of weird. The world is very similar. As far as music and audiences go, it's pretty universal. There's a lot of screaming everywhere — everybody knows how to scream."
Ike: "It varies subtly in just about every country, but it's pretty much the same. There's a much larger pop culture in Europe in general. I think you could say there's a lot more rock in the United States."

47. How many videos has Hanson released?
A total of seven. They include:

MMMBop — directed by Tamra Davis. *MMMBop* was the first time the public saw Isaac, Taylor, and Zac just being themselves — skateboarding (and crashing into one another), jamming together, and just fooling around.

Where's the Love — directed by Tamra Davis, which was shot on location in London.

I Will Come to You — directed by Peter Christopherson. *I Will Come to You* portrays Ike, Tay, and Zac as a glowing superhero trio.

Tulsa, Tokyo, and the Middle of Nowhere — directed by David Silver. *Tulsa, Tokyo, and the Middle of Nowhere* is an eighty-two-minute docuvideo showing the behind-the-scenes mania of just being Hanson.

Weird — directed by Gus Van Sant. *Weird* has the brothers dressed like street musicians hanging out in a New York subway.

River — directed by Al Yankovic. *River* is a *Titanic* parody.

This Time Around — directed by Dave Myers. A performance-based video.

48. In the song "Soldier," who speaks the first few lines?
Taylor: "Those are our two little sisters, Jessica and Avery. That song is based around this story-

book, so we were trying to capture the vibe behind that. It's a unique song."

49. Do Ike, Taylor, and Zac like doing interviews and photo shoots?

It's all part of the business — they have to do it and they usually enjoy themselves. But there are times when it gets a little rough — like the time they did twenty-one interviews in one day! "Photo shoots are more exhausting," Taylor told *Rolling Stone*.

50. What's the best and the worst thing about being famous?

Ike: "We're enjoying most of what goes on, but sometimes we wonder — if it gets any bigger than this, will we be able to live normal lives? It's already at the point where we can't go out without having photographers chase us."

Zac: "We [didn't like that] because we had to have guards with us and that made it more difficult to meet fans. I love talking to the fans and asking them what they really think."

Taylor: "That's one of the most fun things about

doing this job. If we had to stop that, the fun would be over, and there wouldn't be much point in carrying on."

51. What's the worst thing about touring?
Zac: "Sleeping in a bus bed — you wake up with your face stuck to the wall. Pretty scary!"

52. Is there anything about their fans that annoys Hanson?
Not really. They will always tell you that they love their fans and like meeting and talking to them. The only thing that still *does* bother them . . . sometimes . . . is when the fans scream when they are performing. Zac explains, "Sometimes it means we can't hear ourselves."

53. Do the guys ever get nervous while performing onstage?
Zac: "Sorry, that doesn't happen!"
Taylor: "When you first start out, you have a few butterflies when you go onstage. But mostly when you go onstage that's all you're thinking about, so getting nervous doesn't come into the picture."

54. How many hours in a normal day does Hanson spend playing music?

Taylor: "Most of the time there isn't a real normal day — so it's hard to say how much you get to play. When we are recording, we spend most of the day with our music."

Zac: "When we're on tour, we play four or five hours a day."

55. How long did it take for "MMMBop" to become a number-one hit?

"MMMBop" was released to radio stations in March 1997. By May it entered *Billboard*'s Top 100 Pop Singles chart at number sixteen. It took only three weeks for "MMMBop" to become the number-one song in America.

56. Why does Taylor use two keyboards? Are they different?

In concerts, Taylor uses a keyboard that sounds like a piano, which is the sound he likes best, and another keyboard that is an organ. He actually is trying to design a combination module with one keyboard.

57. How many songs did Hanson write for *This Time Around*?

Zac: "We *wrote* about twenty-five songs."

Taylor: "We *recorded* seventeen songs for the record — it was actually really hard for us to pick our favorite songs. It was a hard process to narrow it down to thirteen. It was kind of like telling four of your kids they can't go to Disney World or, 'Sorry, the rest of you have to go jump off a cliff now.'"

58. Was Hanson worried that their old fans might not be there when they released *This Time Around*?

Ike: "That was a thing we were considering, sure. But you just do the best you can and that's all we were doing. It was a while, and you never know how quickly the next record will come together."

59. Did Hanson make a conscious effort to change their sound on *This Time Around*?

Ike: "It wasn't a conscious effort at all."

Taylor: "Just over the three years, it was a natural evolution to rock."

60: Is there anyplace Hanson is looking forward to touring for *This Time Around*?
Ike: "I'm particularly looking forward to going back to Red Rocks."
Zac: "I'm more looking forward to going to places that we haven't [toured extensively, especially] South America — plus all the places that we didn't get to go to before."
Taylor: "As far as Sydney, Australia — we played a concert there in 1999 — that's an amazing city. And we didn't really spend a lot of time in South America, and we have a huge following there."

5
Real & Reel Life

Let's clear up what's true, what's false —
and what Zac says!

**61. When Isaac, Taylor, and Zac are out on
the road, what do they miss most about
home?**
Ike: "I think if you miss anything from home, it's
just the relaxation of being someplace where
you feel very comfortable, and that's all you
really miss. However, we feel very comfortable
onstage because that's where you make your
music. There's just such an incredible feeling
when the fans are out there enjoying your music, you hit that note, the song stops, and

everybody claps and screams and stuff like that."

Zac: "Sleep!"

62. When Zoe was a baby and was on the road with her brothers, did Ike, Taylor, or Zac ever have to change her diapers?

Taylor: "We couldn't avoid it. There are seven kids in our family. What can we do? We've changed a lot of diapers."

63. Did the guys really paint the walls of their home recording studio?

Yes. Actually, that's one of their favorite things to do. Ike says it really relaxes them. He told *Just Entertainment* magazine, "We spent a lot of time painting the walls of our studio. There are actually scenes of that wall in the *Tulsa, Tokyo, and the Middle of Nowhere* video."

64. Has Hanson ever gone out in public in disguises so they wouldn't be recognized?

Ike: "No, not really. We just are ourselves and . . ."

Taylor: ". . . deal with it as we go. There are certain times, like in movie theaters, where you have to sneak in once the lights go down or something like that. It's kind of a joke, but sometimes we'll just go in a really big group or we'll take walkie-talkies. It's almost more fun. . . . You become like a secret agent almost."

65. Is it true that Isaac is writing a science fiction story?

No. In an old interview Ike mentioned that he was writing a story, and somehow it got reported that he was working on a science fiction novel. "I still get asked that a lot," he laughs. "It's not true."

66. What are the weirdest rumors Hanson has heard about themselves?

Taylor: "There are so many rumors that get circulated about us dating people, buying extravagant cars, all kinds of things."

Zac: "One rumor about me was weird — I heard that I was dead! Wild!"

Taylor: "It was very unoriginal; the rumor was

we were all in a car, we were in Paris, we were being chased by paparazzi, and we crashed. Zac died, and Ike and I were in a coma. That was a big deal because it was announced officially on the radio. There's a lot of things, silly little rumors, too, like we're all gonna dye our hair blue."

Zac: "There was one about Ike dating LeAnn Rimes. We don't even *know* LeAnn Rimes."

67. Does Ike still do his Kermit the Frog impression?

He's grown out of that phase, though if you push him, he might give you a sample.

68. Do any of the Hanson guys remember their dreams?

Zac: "I don't usually have dreams. I'm too busy sleeping to dream."

Taylor: "Yeah, me, too. The schedule we're keeping is pretty hectic, so when you sleep, you sleep hard — you're out. Besides, we probably wouldn't reveal our dreams anyway."

69. Did Zac ever want to be anything else besides a musician?
Zac: "I've always liked to draw, so I thought I might become a cartoonist or something."

70. Do the guys in Hanson read all the unofficial books written about them?
Taylor: "A lot of those books are fairly funny, because they make up things you didn't know about yourself. You're, like, 'Huh, I didn't know that. And that. And that.' It definitely gives you a blow to the head; you laugh at it."

71. Has the Hanson family taken a vacation recently?
Well, there hasn't been much time. The guys toured for more than two years straight, then they started to work on songs for *This Time Around*. However, Zac told *Smash Hits* magazine, "We chilled a little bit, we went skiing with the family, but pretty much we didn't stop writing."

72. Is it true that there is going to be a sit-com or movie about Hanson?

Back when Hanson first released *Middle of Nowhere*, there was some discussion about a Brady Bunch-type TV sitcom, but the family quickly nixed that. As for a movie, Zac laughs with a reporter from *Smash Hits*, "I don't really think people want to know about my life. 'He was born and he said, "'Eeuunggahh!'"

73. When the Hanson family left Tulsa in the early 1990s, where did they live?

Trinidad, Venezuela, and Ecuador. Walker Hanson worked for an oil company, and the family spent a little more than a year in these exotic locations.

74. Why did Diana Hanson home-school her kids?

Initially it started when the family moved out of the country for Walker's job, but Diana continued to home school the kids even after they returned to Tulsa. Zac told *US* magazine, "Our mom wanted to home-school us because she wanted to have a better relationship with us."

75. Did the guys miss going to a regular school?
Ike: "Let's see, I missed out on getting dumped by about ten million girls. Getting beat up by bullies. Peer pressure."

76. If Ike, Taylor, and Zac went to the moon, what would they take with them?
Ike: "We'd take our cousin Wayne, because he's, like, our best friend."

Zac: "He's our little toy! And my animal would be my stuffed dog. No, not a real one. I'm not that gross!"

Taylor: "I guess I'd say a dog because they're loyal. But then again, I might take a monkey, like the one in *Indiana Jones* — the little fella would be loads of fun. I'd also take a cute girl!"

77. What's the most mischievous thing Taylor has ever done?
Taylor: "When I was really little, I stole a little

toy like a Transformer from a friend. He didn't get all mad, but he told his mom it was missing."

Ike: "It was kinda my fault that Taylor got found out, because I told on him!"

78. Do Ike, Taylor, or Zac collect souvenirs from the cities they visit all around the world?

Taylor: "Not really. We've got our journals so we can remind ourselves of what happened."

79. How have the group's friends reacted to their success?

Taylor: "Our friends have become part of our fleet now. A lot of times there's so much mail that comes in, we say, 'Let's have a mail-opening party,' and [they come over] and we read 'em."

Ike: "They've been very much into the band and kind of been with us for quite a while. They remember the old records when they weren't being released and stuff like that. It's very cool for us and for them."

80. Is it true that Hanson has started rock climbing?

Taylor: "Yes. We practiced by rock climbing in indoor gyms, and then we worked our way up to real rocks — Joshua Tree and the San Bernadino National Forest. It was a lot of fun. It has amazing views."

81. What's the best advice Hanson's mom, Diana, has ever given them?

When a reporter at a *This Time Around* press conference asked this question, Zac was typical Zac. He answered, "Don't talk to strangers." And then he got up to leave!

82. Is Ike going to college?

Ike: "Well, I'm college-age. I've been auditing some classes here and there, but I'm not, like, going to a university. I've been taking kind of odd subjects. Physics, of all things, and music history."

83. Is it true that Taylor is left-handed and dyslexic?

Taylor doesn't know how that particular rumor got started, but he has explained many times since he first heard it, "I'm right-handed and not dyslexic."

84. When Ike, Taylor, or Zac do something wrong at home, do they still get punished?

Oprah Winfrey asked the guys this when they appeared on her show in February 1998. They admitted that there were times when, if they didn't do their chores and stuff, they did get punished, but according to Taylor, their parents didn't send them to their rooms. "We just had other stuff [to do] that we didn't like."

85. Do any of the Hanson brothers have anything pierced besides their ears — or any tattoos?

No. One time Diana Hanson put her foot down when Ike, Taylor, and Zac were doing a segment for MTV in Los Angeles and Zac insisted he wanted to go to a body-piercing place. But that was just Zac acting like Zac. However, Ike did tell a fan during a 1999 Yahoo! cyberchat that he might consider getting a tattoo or something else. "It's possible, if [I] just felt crazy enough — it depends on how crazy [I] feel at the moment."

86. How long did Ike have to wear his braces?
Three years — they are off now.

87. What made Ike and Taylor decide to cut their hair?
Ike: "I wanted something different. It was one of those things I've been thinking about doing for a while. It took me three years to decide. Partly, it was because I took up surfing in L.A. and it bothered me, but actually, this length is worse for surfing. I can't pull it back anymore. Tay's hair is the worst — it's like a wall in front of him when he surfs."

6
Hanson.com

Find out about Hanson and the world of cybercommunications.

88. What has been the most outrageous E-mail message Hanson has gotten?

Besides marriage proposals and declarations of undying love, the guys think that the most surprising messages were when they cut their hair. They got all sorts of E-mail telling Ike that they weren't mad at him for cutting his hair. They even got phone messages on the Hanson Hotline about Ike's lost locks. Zac laughs in an *Entertainment Weekly* article, "The hotline is to give fans information, and it'd be like, 'Isaac . . .

[sob] . . . we're . . . sup . . . porting . . . you . . . [choking sob] . . . and your haircut!'"

89. Is it true that Hanson has gone into business with rocker David Bowie?

Yes. In March 2000, Ike, Taylor, and Zac announced that they signed on with David Bowie's Internet company to launch their own Internet service provider: Hanson Net. It will cost fans $14.95 a month to subscribe to the service, for which they will be able to get a virtual backstage pass to Hanson. Members will have access to Hanson-customized Web browsers as well as Hanson updates on tour dates, plus audio and video clips, photos, and much, much more. Ike told *USA Today*: "[This] is a great thing to have, to supply information and media to your fans, to be able to activate that fan base, and to give them something extra. . . . We're into the whole Internet service and everything about it. I think there are a lot of opportunities. It's just a really cool tool."

For more info on Hanson Net, check out:

www.hanson.net
www.hansonline.com
www.davidbowie.com

90. How did Hanson celebrate the release of their single "This Time Around"?

On March 31, they had an exclusive on-line listening party. Fans got the "secret" code invite by downloading "This Time Around" from various Web sites — radio stations, MTV, etc. With this passkey, fans were able to join Ike, Taylor, and Zac at the MTV-organized party. *TRL*'s Carson Daly was the host, and he chatted with the guys and their fans in between playing the entire *This Time Around* album. Even Jonny Lang and John Popper stopped by for the festivities.

91. What was the "Build Your Own Hanson Homepage" contest?

Universal Records, Hanson's label, sponsored this contest. They announced the contest on February 15, 2000, on www.hansonline.com, and in less than two weeks they had received close to 10,000 entries. The winners of the homepage contest were special guests of Hanson on their second on-line event, which was scheduled for May 8, 2000.

92. Are Ike, Taylor, and Zac Web surfers?
Taylor: "That's something we are very into. We like going on-line and looking at all the Hanson sites. I think it's cool to go see different sites because that's how you see everybody else's perspective of you and their different ideas about songs and stuff like that."

93. How many hits a day do Hanson's Web sites get?
Right now it's almost impossible to count. In 1997, when they first started, their AOL E-mail address (Mmmbop@AOL.com) got a thousand hits a day. Insiders estimate that if you include www.hansonline.com, www.hanson.net, and the many other avenues to find out information about the group, the figure could be in the millions per day!

7
Fabulous Firsts

Be the first in your class to know these facts!

94. What were the first songs Hanson ever wrote?

Taylor: "The first songs we wrote were about [our brother and sisters]. We wrote a lullaby for Mackenzie called 'I'll Show You Mars.'"

Ike: "Our parents were musical, so I think it was in the genes. I actually wrote my first song when I was in the third grade. . . . The first real song we wrote was called 'Rain,' and it was recorded on our first independent record, *Boomerang*.

We wrote the song at home in our upstairs room on a really cheap keyboard."

95. What was the very first song Hanson ever sang?

Diana and Walker Hanson taught Ike, Taylor, and Zac to sing "Amen" in harmony after saying grace at family meals.

96. What were the first songs Hanson sang when they started performing?

Ike: "We sang original songs that we were writing. And we also performed 1950s and 1960s stuff like 'Johnny Be Good,' 'Splish Splash,' 'Rockin' Robin,' and 'Good Golly Miss Molly.'"

97. What was Isaac's first guitar?

Ike: "The very first guitar was a small classical guitar that I got for Christmas one year. I don't remember how old I was, but I was between eight and eleven years old. I never really played the guitar, just banged on it. Not too long ago I tried to play it, but it doesn't stay in tune. The real playing started when I got a Gibson Les Paul look-alike from a local pawnshop, along with a small thirty-five-watt amp. I was fourteen."

98. Where was Hanson's first official show?
Ike: "There is a yearly arts festival in Tulsa, Olahoma, called Mayfest. It was there at Mayfest in 1992 that we did our first thirty-minute show, completely a cappella."

99. What did Zac buy with his first paycheck?
Zac: "Um, groceries? People think that we got all this money and went out and bought Porsches and Lamborghinis and big mixing boards. We wanted to. But we didn't!"

100. What was the first song that Taylor ever played on the piano?
Taylor: "I think it was 'Mary Had a Little Lamb.' I used to show off how fast I could play it."

101. Will Hanson ever break up?
Taylor: "We want to do it for as long as we can.

Till we can't do it anymore. Till my hands can't physically do it. No matter what, even if everything crashes and burns, at least we enjoyed ourselves and had a passion for our work."

8
Hanson Songfest
Bonus Q + A

Songwriting has been part of Ike, Tay, and Zac's life for almost as long as they can remember. It just comes naturally to them. In a press conference shortly before the release of *This Time Around,* Hanson discussed their songs, writing style, and inspirations.

Hanson on Their Music

Q: What was the writing process you went through for *This Time Around*?

Ike: "The process itself was not particularly different [from before]. You like to think that you get better as you do it more. But I mean, you know, it's just things are different. You write new songs, you come up with different chord ideas, you write in a different key."

Taylor: "I think [*This Time Around*] is definitely taking the next step — as far as just getting a little more rock and roll. Some of the chord structures are a little more complicated, but yeah, you hope you are continuing to improve your craft a little bit. As far as the writing goes, you're just taking a little different perspective on things, on some of the songs."

Q: What were the themes for these songs?

Taylor: "Everything we think and see and experience could be presented in a song. So the experiences of being able to travel and meet people and talk, definitely changes your perspective and could change how you write. It might influence your songwriting. And also just being on the road, a lot of these songs were written while we were traveling, while we were in a hotel room with a little piano."

Ike: "You just evolve naturally. I don't think it's so much directly related to travel or things like that. It's more that as natural evolution goes on, as you experience more, as you do more, you just grow and you change. That's just a natural progression — that's something that happens."

Taylor: "And you never really notice it. People go, 'Wow, you guys have really changed a lot!' And we're like, 'Really? Wow, I didn't notice it.' We were actually listening to *Middle of Nowhere* and we [realized it would] be interesting to see how people respond [to *This Time Around*]. Because if you're only familiar with 'MMMBop' and you haven't really listened through *Middle of Nowhere* ... *This Time Around* is gonna be quite a jump for people."

Q: Was Hanson worried about their new album not being as successful as *Middle of Nowhere* [which sold eight million copies]?

Taylor: "When we set out to make this record, we weren't thinking of anything other than our desire to create songs that we could be proud of.

In the end, we think there are songs here for fans of the last album — and hopefully, songs others will dig as well."

Zac: "This [new album] is the exciting part. This is when we get to share our new songs and see how people respond to them. It's a little scary because we realize that it's pretty much out of our hands now [that the album's out]. We also know that some of this album is not in the pocket of what's currently happening. We're asking people to stretch a little with us."

Isaac: "We're aware that there are no guarantees in this business. So we [were] prepared to give this record all we've got. We're not afraid of hard work. In fact, we thrive on it."

Q: How do you go about writing your songs?

Ike: "It happens in all different ways. . . . It's completely spontaneous."

Taylor: "It can be anything from [one of us] has a lyric he wants to write a song about, or just a melody that comes into his head. Or we're jamming together, just messing around, and a song comes about. Like the first song, 'In the City' — that was all based around this groove that we made up."

Ike: "We were just down in the garage and Tay started goofing around on the keyboards, and I was actually playing bass at the time just for the heck of it."

Taylor: "And in about an hour the song was basically done. So that's one example. But the song 'Runaway Run' was very much like a piece here, a piece there, and it all kind of came together and turned into a song."

Ike: "Every part was completely individual, written completely separately from each other, written for a totally separate song, so all the little sections were not written for that song."

Taylor: "Yeah, there's not really a *way* to write. I wish I could say there's a way to write songs, but there's no formula."

Ike: "In fact you'll find that the hardest writing situations are the ones where you actually have to sit down and say, '[Darn], we *need* to write that second verse to that song.'"

Zac: "What were we thinking? Why didn't we write it in the spur of the moment?"

Ike: "And that's the hardest part — going back to a song and realizing we need to finish these lyrics because they're not quite right."

Q: Any interesting stories behind any of the songs that are on the album?

Ike: "A lot of the songs are oftentimes not really related to direct life experiences. I think 'Bridges of Stone' [a song we cut from the album but will perform live] would be one."

Taylor: "'Bridges of Stone' is a good one. The song 'Wish That I Was There' — we were demo-ing a different song and we were supposed to be working on it. I kept picking up the acoustic gui-tar, playing over the part right before we recorded it; and then all of a sudden I started playing something else. We just completely went off on this song and it just totally came to-gether."

Q: You collaborate with a lot of people on the new album. What was the most exciting collaboration?

Taylor: "There were kind of three main ones: Jonny Lang, John Popper, and Rose Stone and the choir. I mean I think as far as Rose being there, well that was just amazing, because she was the keyboardist for Sly and the Family Stone. She steps in and she just has this aura . . ."

Ike: "She's a very cool person and the group, the choir that she put together . . ."

Taylor: ". . . is just really amazing."

Ike: "You realize just how far you have to go as far as a singer . . ."

Taylor: "That was really cool, a very cool experience, and I think it really added to the album, just kind of the sound overall. The collaborations were a lot of fun."

Q: What did you learn from the collaborations?

Taylor: "I think the biggest thing . . . that we learned was just how to work with [other] people, learning how to give and take and be politically correct also. You have to work with people and make it happen — it's just kind of the life experience of getting through it."

9
The Ultimate
Hanson Fact-o-File

CLARKE ISAAC HANSON

The Basics

Nickname: Ike

Birthday: November 17, 1980

Birthplace: Tulsa, Oklahoma

Hometown: Tulsa, Oklahoma

Parents: Walker and Diana

Siblings: Brothers Taylor, Zachary, and Mackenzie; sisters Jessica, Avery, and Zoe

Astro Sign: Scorpio

Astro Qualities: Scorpio is a water sign — those who are born under this sign can be stubborn, intense, even willful. They are also extremely sensitive, but totally adventurous.

Hair: Blond
Eyes: Dark brown
Height: 5'11"
Righty or Lefty: Right-handed
Shoe Size: 14 men's
Worst Habit: Biting his nails
Instruments: Guitar, piano, vocals
Early Musical Influences: '50s and early '60s rock and roll
Special Talents: Imitates Kermit the Frog, Bullwinkle, and Butt-head
Self-Description: "Stupid goofy"

Faves
Color: Green
Current Music: Counting Crows, Lenny Kravitz, Beck, Macy Gray, Ben Folds Five
Sports: Speed hockey, basketball, rock climbing, and surfing
Food: Italian — especially lasagna and spaghetti; steak
Fast Food: Pizza
Candy: Heath Bar
Ice Cream: Vanilla
Peanut Butter: Crunchy

Item of Clothing: His brown leather jacket
Condiment: Salt
TV Shows: *Seinfeld* reruns, *South Park*
Movies: *Sixteen Candles*, *Star Wars*
Actors: Mel Gibson, Arnold Schwarzenegger, Harrison Ford
School Subject: Science
High-tech Toy: His videocamera
Ways to Relax: Go to the movies
Concert Site: Red Rocks in Colorado

Firsts
On-line listening Party: On March 31, 2000, MTV and Carson Daly hosted the very first on-line full album listening party for Hanson's album *This Time Around*.
Original Song: "I actually wrote my first song when I was in third grade."

JORDAN TAYLOR HANSON

The Basics
Nickname: Tay
Birthday: March 14, 1983
Birthplace: Tulsa, Oklahoma

Hometown: Tulsa, Oklahoma

Parents: Walker and Diana

Siblings: Brothers Isaac, Zachary, and Mackenzie; sisters Jessica, Avery, and Zoe

Astro Sign: Pisces

Hair: Blond

Eyes: Blue

Height: 6'

Righty or Lefty: Right-handed

Dimple: He has one on his right cheek

Instruments: Keyboard, bongos — lead singer

Early Musical Influences: Chuck Berry, Bobby Darin, and the Beach Boys

Special Talent: He draws cartoon characters

Self-Description: "The quiet one"

Coolest Places Visited: New Orleans, Los Angeles, London, New York — "We really enjoyed being in New York. We had a whole two-day tour — and we walked up the Statue of Liberty."

Words to Live By: "Everything changes."

Weird Fact: There is a fan group on the Internet called "The Taylor Hanson Cult."

Faves

Color: Red

Sports: Speed hockey, basketball, soccer, Rollerblading, surfing, and rock climbing

Pastimes: Drawing and reading

Food: Burritos, steak, chicken, fish, cheeseburgers with everything, and mashed potatoes

Fast Food: McDonald's

Breakfast Cereal: Cocoa Puffs

Dessert: His mom's brownies

Candy: Red jelly beans

Ice Cream: Strawberry

Drink: Bottled water

Soda: Dr Pepper, Mugs Rootbeer

Singers: Counting Crows, Black Crowes, Sheryl Crow, Beck, Lenny Kravitz, Lauryn Hill

Style of Clothes: Comfortable T-shirts and jeans

Item of Clothing: His black leather jacket

Brand of Shoes: Adidas, Doc Martens

Computer: Toshiba laptop

Store: Gap

Actor: Tom Cruise

Actress: Jennifer Aniston

Movie: *Star Wars*
Sports Team: Miami Dolphins

Firsts
Piercings: Tay had the top part of his left ear pierced — "Right through the tough bit. A warning to anyone who's thinking of getting it done — the pain never ends!"

ZACHARY WALKER HANSON

The Basics
Nicknames: Zac; Animal (from the Muppets' character)
Birthday: October 22, 1985
Birthplace: Tulsa, Oklahoma
Hometown: Tulsa, Oklahoma
Parents: Walker and Diana
Siblings: Brothers Isaac, Taylor, and Mackenzie; sisters Jessica, Avery, and Zoe
Astro Sign: Libra
Hair: Blond
Eyes: Brown

Height: 5'9"

Righty or Lefty: Left-handed

Instrument: Drums

Drum Brand: Pearl

Early Musical Influences: '50s and early '60s rock and roll

Special Talent: He's a master skateboarder

Self-Description: "The romantic one and the goofy, funny one"

Worst Habit: Burping — he can do it on cue.

Faves

Color: Blue

Sports: Dirt biking, paintballing, skiing, surfing, and rock climbing

Pastime: Drawing

School Subject: Math

Food: Lasagna, hot dogs, pizza

Fast Food: McDonald's

Ice Cream: Chocolate

Drink: Dr Pepper

Item of Clothing: His cargo pants

Store: Gap

Way to Relax: Sleep — "[I can] sleep for twelve hours a day!"
Video Game: GoldenEye

Firsts
"If Only": Zac's favorite song on *This Time Around* was the first single released in Australia

10
Where & How to Contact Hanson

The Official Hanson Fanzine:

MOE

www.hansonline.com

Universal Records Address: Hanson
Island Def Jam Music
Group
Worldwide Plaza
825 Eighth Avenue
New York, NY 10019

or

Hanson
Island Def Jam Music Group
11159 Santa Monica Blvd.

Suite 1000
Los Angeles, CA 90025
or
Hanson Management
 Company Address: Hanson
                          c/o Triune Music Group
                          8322 Livingston Way
                          Los Angeles, CA 90046

Official Hanson Phone Hotline: (918) 446-3979*

*This is a toll call — ask your parents for permission
first.

Official Internet Access

Official Hanson Web Site:
http://www.hansonline.com

Fan Club E-Mail Address:
hansonfans@hansonline.com

Official Hanson ISP:

www.hanson.net
(The ISP costs $14.95 per month and features chats with Hanson, digital photos, rehearsal footage, audio-video, and special ticket offers — a "virtual backstage pass.")

Island Def Jam Music Group Web Site:
http://www.umusic.com.artists/hanson/
hanson_homepage.html